Living in Harsh Lands

By Richard C. Lawrence

CELEBRATION PRESS

Pearson Learning Group

The following people from **Pearson Learning Group**
have contributed to the development of this product:

Dorothea Fox, Joan Mazzeo **Design** | **Editorial** Leslie Feierstone-Barna, Cindy Kane
Christine Fleming **Marketing** | **Publishing Operations** Jennifer Van Der Heide
Production Laura Benford-Sullivan
Content Area Consultant Amy Keller

The following people from **DK** have
contributed to the development of this product:

Art Director Rachael Foster

Martin Wilson **Managing Art Editor** | **Managing Editor** Marie Greenwood
Polly Appleton **Design** | **Editorial** Selina Wood
Brenda Clynch **Picture Research** | **Production** Gordana Simakovic
Richard Czapnik, Andy Smith **Cover Design** | **DTP** David McDonald
Consultant David Green

Dorling Kindersley would like to thank: Rose Horridge, Hayley Smith, and Gemma Woodward in the DK Picture Library;
Simon Mumford for cartography; Penny Smith for editorial assistance; Johnny Pau for additional cover design work.

Picture Credits: Bryan And Cherry Alexander Photography: 17cr, 17bl, 31. Chris Bonington Picture Library: 29b. Corbis: Tiziana and
Gianni Baldizzone 15b. Sue Cunningham Photographic: SCP 20cr, 20br, 21tr. DK Images: American Museum of Natural History 23tr;
Stephen Hayward 12cr. Ffotograff: Nick Tapsell 19cl. Hutchison Library: 10br, 11br, 30tl; Dirk R. Frans 1cr, 25cl, 25b; Jeremy A. Horner 30b;
Brian Moser 22b; Angela Silvertop 4; Isabella Tree 1cl. Gables Travel: 19br. Lonely Planet Images: Clem Lindenmayer 1r, 26b; Eric L. Wheater 28br.
Nativestock.com: Marilyn 'Angel' Wynn 23cl, 23b. N.H.P.A.: David Middleton 13t. Oxford Scientific Films: Alain Cristof 26cr. Panos Pictures: 18b,
21cr; B. Klass 24b; John Miles 11cr; Sean Sprague 6b; Penny Tweedie 11t. Pictures Colour Library: 1l, 5b, 19t.
South American Pictures: Tony Morrison 27b. Still Pictures: Mark Edwards 21b. World Pictures: 12b, 29cr.
Jacket: Corbis: Jacques Langevin front bl; Francoise de Mulder front t.

All other images: 🔲 Dorling Kindersley © 2005. For further information see www.dkimages.com

ISBN: 0-7652-5258-9

Color reproduction by Colourscan, Singapore
Printed in the United States of America
2 3 4 5 6 7 8 9 10   08 07 06 05

1-800-321-3106
www.pearsonlearning.com

Contents

Introduction

Some people live in the hottest, coldest, wettest, and driest parts of the planet. People of different **cultures**, or ways of life, learn to adapt to the harsh or extreme climates in which they live. A group's culture includes all of its beliefs, customs, and traditions. Types of food, dwellings, tools, and occupations are also part of a culture.

This book will introduce you to a variety of cultures, from those of the tropical rain forest to those of the frozen Arctic tundra. You can learn how people have adapted to such extreme environments by making the best use of the resources around them. You can also discover how they have adjusted to life in the modern world while preserving their cultural traditions.

The Bedouins thrive in the extremely hot, dry climate of the desert.

Life in Hot, Dry Lands

About one-third of Earth's land is hot and dry. This land includes **deserts**, **semideserts**, and **savannahs**. These lands present challenges to all forms of life.

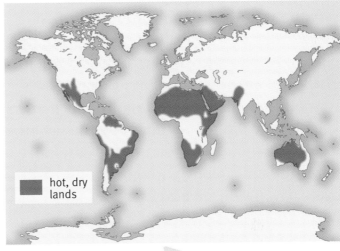

Map showing the major hot semideserts, deserts, and savannahs of the world

With less than 10 inches of rain a year, deserts are the driest places on Earth. Desert animals and plants have adapted to dry conditions. Camels, scorpions, and sand vipers, for example, conserve moisture and avoid the heat of the day. Desert plants, such as cacti, hold water in their stems or roots.

Semideserts, such as those found in Australia, have about 15 inches of rainfall a year. Semideserts support a little more vegetation than deserts. These plants make it possible for people living there to raise some livestock, such as sheep and goats.

Savannahs receive between 20 and 50 inches of rain a year. These areas are ideal for grazing animals.

The Negev desert, Israel

The Masai

Many Masai (mah-SY) live on the hot savannahs of Kenya and Tanzania, in East Africa. They are one of the few groups to live peacefully with the wildlife of the savannah. The Masai are often thought of mainly as warriors, but are in fact primarily cow herders.

Map showing where the Masai people live

There are limited resources on the savannah, so the Masai use every part of the cows they herd. The milk, along with goat's milk, is drunk every day. Cattle are also used as a source of meat. Their hides are used for clothing. Even their dung is used to construct buildings and provide fuel for fires. Because of their usefulness and their cultural value, cattle traditionally have been given as gifts for births, initiations, and marriages.

Early Masai were **nomads**. They herded their cattle across the Great Rift Valley. They migrated to avoid overgrazing or to search for a better water supply. Because their dwellings were relatively easy to construct, they simply abandoned them, and moved to a better place.

Masai herding cattle in Kenya

In the 1800s, Europeans took over Masai land for farms, ranches, and parks. The Masai fought for their land rights but eventually lost two-thirds of their territory. Many were squeezed into the least fertile areas of their homeland. Without the land and resources to raise cattle, the Masai faced even more difficulty surviving the harsh climate. Despite efforts to convince them to settle, most Masai are still nomadic.

The Masai have been unwilling to abandon their traditional culture. The loss of land has brought extreme poverty. As a result, some Masai have moved to cities.

The Masai who work in businesses and government maintain some of their traditional culture. Some Masai now own camps and guest ranches on the savannahs. They welcome tourists to join them on safaris. Money from these businesses helps the Masai maintain their land and traditions.

Beaded necklaces are part of the traditional Masai dress.

Rite of Passage

To attain manhood, a Masai youth traditionally had to kill a lion single-handedly with a spear. The government of Kenya has outlawed this practice.

The permanent home of a Masai family is made from wooden poles covered with dry cow dung, with a grass roof.

The Bedouins

The Bedouins (BED-oo-ihns) are Arabic-speaking nomads who live in the deserts of the Middle East and northern Africa. These desert climates present the Bedouins with the challenges of extreme heat and cold, little water, sandstorms, and sun glare. Bedouins have adapted to the harsh climates by traveling with herds of camels, horses, sheep, and goats in search of grass and water.

Map showing the deserts where the Bedouin people live

For shelter, the Bedouins weave tents of goat hair. The goat hair absorbs and reflects the warmth of the sun while keeping the inside of the tent cool. When the weather is cold or wet, the goat hair acts as insulation, keeping in the warmth of a fire. The tents are simple to erect and dismantle and are easy to carry. This is a necessity for the nomadic lifestyle.

Looping sheep's wool onto a spindle

Bedouins find shelter from the harsh sun in tents.

Bedouin women are known for their spinning and weaving. They use the hair from the herd animals to produce colorfully dyed tent cloths, cushion covers, curtains, and rugs. Bedouins make their clothing to suit the climate. The traditional Bedouin men wear a long, white tunic and a head cloth in the hottest months. These clothes reflect the bright sunlight and protect against blowing sand.

Many Bedouins have given up their traditional lifestyle. The government of Saudi Arabia, for example, has encouraged Bedouins to settle in towns and cities. Some live in apartments and work in the oil industry. Many Bedouin men wear sports coats and trousers rather than the traditional tunic and head cloth.

Despite these changes, many of the 5 million Bedouins in the Middle East still live a partially nomadic life. A family that spends most of the year in a city house may live in a tent for the summer. Some Bedouins also use their traditional skills in new ways. Bedouin men, who are highly skilled trekkers and climbers, often serve as guides and park rangers. Many Bedouin women earn money by selling traditional hand-woven goods in city markets. Used to adapting to the harsh climate of the desert, the Bedouins have proved they can also adapt to living in cities.

Many Bedouin children wear modern clothes.

Traditionally, Bedouins have traveled through the desert on camels. Some now drive trucks.

9

Aboriginal Australians

Originally, the **indigenous** people of Australia lived in about 500 different groups. Each had its own language and traditions. At first, most lived along the coast, but gradually, some of the people spread into the interior desert regions of Australia called the outback.

The Aboriginal people, who make up 2 percent of the population, live in these regions.

The Aboriginal people were hunters and gatherers. They invented tools that had many uses. The boomerang was a clever hunting weapon. If it did not hit its target, it circled around and returned to the thrower. That saved energy in the hot, dry outback. The spear thrower made spears fly farther and also served as a knife and a fire igniter.

Boomerangs were originally used as a hunting weapon.

The Aboriginal people moved from place to place in the bush to find food and water. Snakes, witchetty grubs, and small mammals such as bandicoots were part of the people's diet. Women ground up grass seeds between stones to make small flat cakes. The Aboriginal people learned how to locate water in deep, hidden springs and to dig up sweet roots to quench their thirst.

Bush food: bush onion, gabiny fruits, and damper bread

Aboriginal dancers

Around campfires, Aboriginal people told stories of the Dreamtime. This was the time when their ancestor spirits created the world. For thousands of years, the Aboriginal people have made paintings of the Dreamtime on rocks and have drawn patterns in the sand to trace their ancestors' journeys. For many Aboriginal people today, the Dreamtime is an important belief.

Rock art painting of the Lightning Brothers, spirits from the Dreamtime

Today, most of Australia's 250,000 Aboriginal people live in cities and towns. They have achieved success in modern Australia while maintaining their cultural identity. For many years, the Aboriginal people were denied some basic rights. In the 1960s, new laws helped them to gain the right to vote and to receive better housing, jobs, and education. They still struggle to regain land taken from them during early European settlement.

Aboriginal doctor with patient

Life in Cold Lands

In the far south of the Southern Hemisphere lies Antarctica, a continent equal in size to Europe and the United States combined. The temperature of Antarctica never rises above freezing, 32 degrees Fahrenheit. About 98 percent of the land is covered by ice.

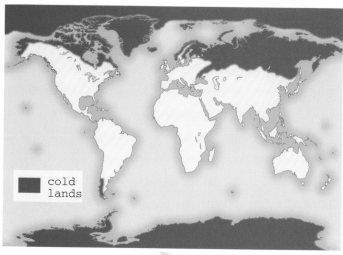

cold lands

The climate of this continent supports many plants and animals. Lichens, algae, and mosses grow in low-lying clusters. By staying close together and near the ground, the plants can trap moisture, block wind, and avoid being crushed by the snow.

Although some plants can survive the cold climate, there is not enough vegetation to support land mammals. The coast, however, close to the fish- and nutrient-rich ocean, is home to seals and walruses. Birds are plentiful, too, including the kelp gull, the albatross, and the giant petrel. The flightless penguin is Antarctica's best-known bird.

Map showing the cold lands of the world

Mosses and lichens can survive in extremely low temperatures.

Penguins on an iceberg in the Weddell sea, Antarctica

The tundra landscape of northwest Canada

In the far north of the Northern Hemisphere, the Arctic Ocean is a sea of packed ice and icebergs. Arctic lands include parts of Canada, Alaska, the Russian Federation, Greenland, Iceland, Sweden, and Norway. Although the Arctic temperature can rise as high as 50 degrees Fahrenheit, much of this region is frozen year-round. The polar bear is the only land mammal that travels over the Arctic ice. These white bears hunt seals that live in the icy ocean.

Tundra is treeless land surrounding the Arctic Ocean at the northern edges of Europe, Asia, and North America. Tundra soil is frozen as far as 20 inches below the surface. This frozen soil is called **permafrost**. When the surface thaws in summer, grasses and flowers briefly bloom.

Migratory birds feed and breed on the tundra each summer. Land mammals, including the Arctic fox and wolf, live on the tundra. Their thick coats and sheltered dens help them survive the polar winters. Large animals, such as moose, musk oxen, and caribou (also known as reindeer) graze there. Swarms of insects survive there, too, and often plague the grazing herds.

Arctic wolves hunt in packs and mostly eat caribou.

The Saami

The Saami (SAH-mee) are an indigenous people of far northern Europe. Originally, the Saami were hunters, fishers, and gatherers. They survived in the cold, harsh climates by using the resources they found there. Fish were plentiful on the coast, and abundant beaver and wild reindeer were hunted on land. In fact, the growth of the wild reindeer population in the sixteenth and seventeenth centuries changed Saami culture. Instead of simply hunting the animals, the Saami began trapping and taming them to increase their herds. Because their herds grew so large, the Saami had to move from place to place to find good grazing lands.

Map showing where the Saami people live

In the seventeenth century, reindeer became extremely valuable. They were used for pulling sleds as well as for their hides, meat, and milk. The Saami language has more than twenty different words for reindeer, showing just how important the animal is to this culture.

Polar Night

In the far north, the sun stays below the horizon for months. This is called *kaamos*, or "polar night." In some places polar night lasts as long as six months, followed by six months of continuous daylight, or "polar day."

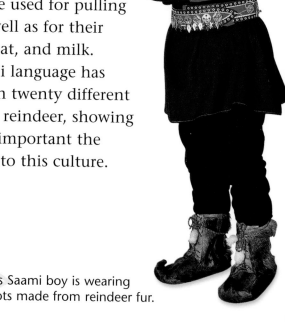

This Saami boy is wearing boots made from reindeer fur.

Over the centuries, Saami lands became divided among Norway, Sweden, Finland, and Russia. This division prevented the Saami from moving along traditional herding routes. As a result, the Saami gradually became more settled.

Like many Saami homes, this house contains a sauna.

Fewer than 75,000 Saami live in Europe's northernmost regions today. In Norway and Sweden, only Saami are allowed to herd reindeer. By law, they must keep the reindeer in enclosed areas for grazing. Saami families now live in one place and herd their animals to new pastures each autumn, using snowmobiles or helicopters. Despite changes in the laws that affect their lives, many Saami continue to practice old traditions. For example, when their first teeth appear, many Saami children are given their first reindeer.

Schools, newspapers, magazines, and a radio station keep Saami language and culture alive. Today, about 40 percent of Saami live by herding, hunting, and fishing—traditional livelihoods. Tourism provides income for many. Others sell *duoji*—crafts such as bonework, antlerwork, and lace.

Saami women weaving colorful cloth on a loom

The Inuit and the Yu'pik

Inuit people
Yu'pik people

Map showing where the Inuit and Yu'pik peoples live

The Inuit (IHN-oo-it) of Canada and Greenland and the Yu'pik Eskimo of southern Alaska live in the cold Arctic region. Traditionally, these Native Americans were nomads, hunting sea mammals, caribou, and fish. These animals provided food, materials for shelter, fuel, tools, weapons, and clothing.

In winter, the Inuit and the Yu'pik traveled over the snow on dogsleds to hunt and to ice fish. They built igloos—round snow houses—as temporary shelters. In their home villages, permanent shelters were made of whalebone, wood, earth, and stone. In summer, the native peoples of the North lived in animal-skin tents.

Whatever the Inuit and the Yu'pik needed, they made themselves. Their traditional kayaks, harpoons, and fur clothing were both durable and beautiful. To save scarce fuel, they often ate fish and meat raw. Eating raw meat also provided them with nutrients that cooking destroys.

Sled dogs are still used for racing and sometimes for work.

Inuit and Yu'pik children dressed for winter

Today, Inuit and Yu'pik cultures combine traditional and modern elements. Many Inuit and Yu'pik now live in towns, where their wooden houses are built on stilts above the snow. This helps to keep their homes warm. At school, children learn their native languages as well as their local languages. Parents may work in the mining, oil, and fishing industries. Many adults keep alive the traditional art of bone and stone carving. These sculptures are popular in art galleries and shops around the world.

The Inuit and the Yu'pik people continue to hunt and fish. However, they are more likely to use snowmobiles and vehicles with outboard motors than dogsleds and kayaks. They still enjoy eating caribou, moose, and duck, but they might flavor them with a little ketchup or mustard. *Agutak*—a traditional iced dessert made with oils, berries, sugar, and water—is still a popular treat.

This soapstone carving is an example of traditional Inuit craft.

Arctic peoples use snowmobiles for activities ranging from hunting to shopping.

The iced dessert known as *agutak*

Life in Wet Lands

Wet lands are the opposite of deserts in many ways. They have high rainfall and moist soil. These areas, such as rain forests and swamps, have abundant plant and animal life.

Tropical rain forests lie in a worldwide belt near the equator. The Amazon region, in South America, is one of the world's largest rain forests. Rain forests are wet and warm year-round. At least half the world's plant and animal species live in rain forests.

The canopy, or top layer, of the Amazon rain forest is thick with leaves, fruit, and flowers. Monkeys, squirrels, fruit bats, and toucans live and feed in the canopy, whereas eagles fly through, scanning for prey. Snakes crawl on tree trunks and branches. Small wild cats, such as clouded leopards and margays, hunt in the trees. Big cats—jaguars and tigers—prowl the rain forest floor.

wet lands

Map showing the rain forests and swamps of the world

The Amazon rain forest covers a vast area—over a billion acres.

18

Swamps are lowlands covered with slow-moving water. They are found in temperate, or mild, climates and in tropical ones. The Everglades is a swamp that covers about 2,746 square miles in southern Florida, in the United States.

The Florida Everglades is home to alligators, snakes, and birds.

The vegetation in a swamp provides nesting and feeding grounds for water birds, such as ducks and herons. Mammals as small as the beaver and as large as the hippopotamus live in swamps, as do countless reptiles, amphibians, and fish.

A **flood plain** is the flat land along a river that floods periodically when the river level rises. Floods deposit mineral-rich sediment, making the plain fertile. Many plants grow in flood plains.

Rice grows abundantly in the flood plains at Guilin, China.

Hippopotamuses live in the rivers and swamps of Africa, taking refuge from the hot sun.

The Yanomami

Several peoples make their home in the Amazon rain forest. Here, the 27,000 Yanomami (yah-NOH-mom-ee) have kept their traditional way of life. These native people use the rain forest and its resources to best benefit both the people and the land.

Map showing where the Yanomami people live

The Yanomami are hunters and gatherers as well as farmers. They burn a small patch of jungle to create a field. In that field, many different plants are grown for food and medicine. After a few years, the soil begins to lose its nutrients. At the beginning of the soil's decline, the Yanomami leave it fallow, or unplanted. Each cleared patch is then given ten to fifty years to rest and regrow while the farmers move on to clear new fields. This type of farming is called **shifting cultivation**.

A Yanomami man felling trees to clear land for crops

However, modern restrictions on land use are causing problems for shifting cultivation. The Yanomami do not have access to enough land to allow for proper regrowth. Thus, the soil becomes depleted, and the rain forest is permanently damaged and destroyed.

A large Yanomami house (top right) with a newly cleared patch of forest nearby

The Yanomami have traditionally depended on hunting and fishing with spears and bows and arrows. As more of the rain forest is lost, however, the animals that the Yanomami hunt, such as deer, monkeys, and tapirs, are more difficult to find. In 1992,

A traditional Yanomami home, known as a *yano*

to protect the Yanomami, the Brazilian government set aside about 23.2 million acres of land as a Yanomami reserve.

Each Yanomami community lives in a ring-shaped group house called a *yano*. In the center of the yano, each family has its own hearth, and hammocks for sleeping. The people have no written language. Instead, they use chants and stories to preserve their history and entertain themselves.

The Yanomami are proud of their culture and believe everything on the land is sacred. They also believe their fate is linked to the environment. If they use the land around them wisely, they reason, the land in turn will take care of them.

A Yanomami family relaxing in its hearth

A Yanomami child with a spear

The Seminole

The Seminole (SEM-ihn-ohl) people are a Native American group who live mostly in Florida. In 1819, the United States acquired Florida from Spain and attempted to remove the Seminole from the land. This attempt resulted in years of war. Many Seminole were marched west to modern-day Oklahoma and placed on reservations. However, most managed to stay in Florida.

Map showing the Everglades region where the Seminole live

During this time, American soldiers hunted the Seminole, who hid in the Everglades. They lived by hunting and fishing. Because they often needed to flee, the Seminole developed houses that could be built and taken down quickly. They found that leaves from palmetto trees, which grew all around, made a good thatch roof over a cypress log frame. They could easily put up these homes on swampy ground or rebuild them after a hurricane.

These Seminole people are thatching the roof of a *chikee,* or house.

Even though the need for flight has ended, some Florida Seminole continue to live in the traditional houses. They support themselves by selling traditional crafts. Seminole use palmetto fiber to make cotton-stuffed dolls in colorfully striped outfits. They sell the dolls, as well as clothing, paintings, and grass baskets to tourists.

Brightly colored Seminole dolls are still made today and are sold to tourists.

Seminole people retain many aspects of their traditional culture. At harvest time, for example, they perform the Green Corn Dance. This is a time to settle tribal disputes and mark the coming of age of young people. Because there is no written language, storytelling also remains central to the Seminole heritage.

The Green Corn Dance

The Seminole tribal government, created in 1957, is strong and dedicated to progress. One of its concerns is keeping the Everglades clean and unspoiled. To preserve its environment and identity, the Seminole nation has created a plan to improve water quality, remove pollutants, and control floods.

The Seminole run tours to teach people about their history and the Everglades environment.

The Bangladeshis

Bangladesh (bang-luh-DESH), a low-lying country east of India, is densely populated. Most of Bangladesh is formed from the **delta** of two great rivers, the Ganges and the Brahmaputra. From June to October, the **monsoon** season brings heavy rains that flood Bangladesh's rivers and delta land. The silt left behind when the water recedes makes the land fertile for farming. The flooding, however, endangers people and crops. During the heavy monsoon of 1998, for example, 30 million Bangladeshis lost their homes to floods.

To avoid flooding, many homes in the delta are built on tall stilts. Boats and rafts carry goods to market. Boats are so important in Bangladesh that boat songs, called *bhatiali*, are one of the most popular types of music.

Map showing where the Bangladeshi people live

Many Bangladeshi houses are built on stilts to protect them from floods.

Agriculture in Bangladesh is limited to plants that thrive in a wet environment. Jute, the country's major export, grows well on the flood plain. This tough, fibrous plant is used to make burlap (tough fabric) and rope. Rice is the leading food crop, and legumes (beans) are second. Fish, readily available in the rivers, is the chief source of animal protein for most Bangladeshis.

The fibrous plant, jute, is used to make rope.

Life in the wet lands of Bangladesh is not easy. Roads and railroads are difficult to build and maintain. Bangladesh cannot afford to build bridges, so slow ferryboats are used to cross most waterways. Major construction and flood-control projects are needed to help ease the challenges of living and farming in the delta.

Bangladeshi children catching fish with nets

Ferries are one of the main forms of transportation in Bangladesh and are often very crowded.

Life in Mountainous Lands

Strong winds, thin air, cold nights, and rugged terrain make mountain life difficult. Mountain animals must be able to keep their balance on steep slopes. They also need thick fur to survive the cold winds. Many birds—especially birds of prey—thrive in mountains.

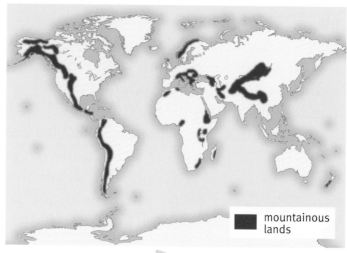

mountainous lands

Map showing the mountainous regions of the world

Plant life varies with the altitude. Deciduous trees—trees that lose their leaves each year—may grow at the foot of a mountain. Higher up, where it is colder, evergreen forests grow. Above the tree line, bogs and meadows appear. Higher still, bare rock is often capped with snow.

Traditionally, mountain peoples herd animals. The goats of the European Alps, the yaks of Asia's Himalayas, and the llamas of South America's Andes are a few examples of these animals.

The agile ibex can scramble over craggy rocks with ease.

The mountainous terrain of the Swiss Alps

The Aymara

The Andes Mountains stretch for 4,970 miles down the Pacific coast of South America. This is the longest mountain range in the world. In the landlocked nation of Bolivia, a high plain called the Altiplano (ahl-tee-PLAH-noh) runs between two chains of the Andes. The Altiplano is cold, dry, windy, and almost treeless. However, almost three-quarters of Bolivia's population live there. Many of them are Aymara (eye-mah-RAH)—an ancient people who have always lived in the mountains.

Map showing where the Aymara people live

Aymara farmers plowing in the Altiplano region

Despite the poor land quality and harsh climate, many Aymara farm on the Altiplano. Family members work together to break up the ground, plant, and harvest. The food crop that grows best on the high plains is the potato, which is native to South America. Barley and wheat are also important crops.

A family may also raise cows, sheep, pigs, chickens, and rabbits. Llamas, native to the Andes, are pack animals used for transport, clothing, fuel, and food. In such a harsh climate, the people must know how to put every resource to its best use.

Like most other indigenous peoples, many Aymara have moved from their traditional homes to towns and cities, such as La Paz, Bolivia's capital. Many Aymara like to watch soccer on television or take bus trips into town. Aymara children in village schools usually study both Spanish and the Aymara language and culture.

These Aymara girls are wearing wool hats and layers of clothes to protect them from cold winds.

Mountain Music

The music of the Andes is known worldwide. Reed panpipes, called *chuqui*, are often the only instruments in an Aymara village band.

Llamas are used to transport goods.

The Sherpa

The Himalayas are the world's tallest mountains. The Himalayan range stretches 1,550 miles from east to west across Asia, mostly in northern India, Nepal, and Bhutan. Mount Everest, the world's highest peak, is in the Himalayas.

The valleys and lower slopes of the Himalayas are well populated. However, only a few hardy groups live in these high altitudes. One of these groups is the Sherpa of Nepal.

The cold, dry climate, as well as the limited resources, require the Sherpa to plan wisely. Most Sherpas live in small farming villages in houses made of stone, mud, and thatch for roofs. Like the Aymara, Sherpas grow crops that thrive in high altitudes, such as potatoes, barley, wheat, and maize (corn). The Sherpa also use yaks, shaggy-haired relatives of oxen, as plow animals. Yaks are a source of milk, meat, and leather.

Map showing where the Sherpa people live

CHINA

Mount Everest
29,035 ft
(8,850 m)

NEPAL

BHUTAN

Sherpa people

INDIA

BANGLADESH

Brahmaputra R.

0 km 100
0 miles 100

Ganges River

A traditional Sherpa house

Yaks and herders at their camp

These Sherpas are porters for a tourist expedition.

If you were to climb high into the Himalayas, you would probably suffer from mountain sickness. The lack of oxygen in the air would make you dizzy, and you might pass out. The Sherpa, however, are used to the thin air. They have physically adapted to their environment. Because of this, many Sherpas become guides and porters for mountain-climbing expeditions. Sherpas are usually included in the groups that climb Mount Everest. In 1953, Sherpa Tenzing Norgay and Sir Edmund Hillary were the first people to reach the top of the world's highest mountain.

Saturday is market day in Namche Bazaar, the main town in the Sherpa region. The town can only be reached on foot.

Conclusion

Throughout the world, indigenous peoples have adapted to harsh climates and terrain. They have made full use of the resources, plants, and animals that are available to them. In their struggle to survive, they have shown great ingenuity and creativity.

With the spread of modern civilization, people living in harsh lands continue to adapt. Most have used modern tools to make life easier. Others who have lost their land have found work in the modern economy. Generally, however, traditional customs and activities survive. In this way, the peoples of harsh lands maintain a living link to their past.

Glossary

cultures   ways of life, including beliefs, customs, and traditions

delta   a deposit of sand and soil that collects at the mouth of a river

deserts   dry regions, usually receiving less than 10 inches of rain a year

flood plain   land that is periodically flooded by a river

indigenous   native to or first in an area

monsoon   winds in southern Asia that bring months of heavy rain

nomads   people who move from place to place

permafrost   frozen soil

savannahs   grasslands with few or no trees

semideserts   dry regions that receive about 15 inches of rainfall a year

shifting cultivation   a farming method by which forest land is cleared and planted for a few years and then left fallow as the farmers move to new fields

swamps   lowlands that are covered with slow-moving water

tropical rain forests   thick forests in the warm regions around the equator that receive frequent heavy rain

tundra   the treeless land surrounding the Arctic Ocean at the northern edges of Europe, Asia, and North America